My Food My Health

A Nurse's Guide to a Healthy Lifestyle

Laurel Woodstock

My Food My Health: A Nurses Guide to a Healthy Lifestyle: Authored by Laurel Woodstock.

Copyright: ©Laurel Woodstock 2023

Edited by Marcia M Publishing House Editorial Team, cover design Marcia M Publishing House.

Published by Marcia M Spence of Marcia M Publishing House Ltd. On behalf of Laurel Woodstock, In West Bromwich, West Midlands, the UNITED KINGDOM B71.

All rights reserved 2023 Laurel Woodstock.

Laurel Woodstock asserts the moral right to be identified as the author of this work. The opinions expressed in this published work are those of the author and do not reflect the opinions of Marcia M Publishing House or its editorial team.

This book is sold subject to the conditions it is not, by way of trade or otherwise, lent, hired out or otherwise circulated in any form of binding or cover other than that in which it is published. No part of this publication may be reproduced, stored in a retrieval system or transmitted in any form or by any means (electronic, mechanical, photocopying, recording or otherwise) without prior written permission from the Author or Publisher.

A copy of this publication is legally deposited in The British Library.

ISBN: 978-1-913905-29-3

www.marciampublishing.com

Contents

About The Author 4

Introduction 7

Part One: Carbohydrates 19

Part Two: Proteins 30

Part Three: Fat 36

Part Four: Vitamins 48

Part Five: Minerals 57

Part Six: Exercise & Rest 69

Part Seven: Epilogue 84

Quick Personal Assessment 99

ABOUT THE AUTHOR

Laurel Woodstock is conscientious, innovative, highly motivated Registered Nurse, A Pastor, and an Ecumenical Chaplain within the NHS. Awarded a Post Graduate Certificate in Public Health.

Founder/project manager for **BREAD** for life Community-based Health Project. The ethos for the project encapsulates:

Building relationships to enhance health and wellbeing.

Restoring and connecting with under-served communities.

Engaging with health providers through partnership working.

Applying knowledge gained to manage healthy lifestyles.

Dieting to balance healthy lifestyles and aim to hydrate with plenty of water.

Laurel had coordinated and hosted various virtual Health Promotion seminars during covid-19 to the present. Her passion is to keep the public abreast of health issues and services available to support them.

Above all, she is an Ambassador of Christ, a wife, a mother, and a grandmother, promoting the message of **HOPE** by:

Holding onto God's Word to be relevant.

Occupying the mission field to be relational.

Pursuing souls as she reimagines God at work in the life of nations that she is witnessing to.

Endeavouring to be rewarded with Eternal a. Everlasting Life; as she is learning from God's word: To number her days that she may gain a heart of wisdom (Psalm 90:12 NKJV)

INTRODUCTION

Tell me what you eat, and I will tell you who you are.

Anthelme Brillat-Savarin, 1755 – 1826

The concept *you are what you eat,* certainly relates to the title and purpose for this book. The title **My Food My Health,** emanates from a group of Christian ladies in leadership roles who had asked me to give a keynote lecture on this subject. As they embarked on their theme, it became apparent that those ladies had the interest of the health of the nation at heart and not just the people whom they were leading. This title for me strikes a balance between:

- ✓ What we eat
- ✓ Why we eat
- ✓ When we eat
- ✓ How we eat

The preceding points characterise the purpose for which this book is written. From my professional background as a Health Practitioner and with the desire to lead by example: **My Food My Health** is a wake-up call for me to personally acknowledge the following:

- ✓ What I eat
- ✓ The benefits gained from what I eat
- ✓ The complications that may manifest in my body if I do not balance what I eat.

Consequently, I have catalogued this book into six main sections:

- ✓ Carbohydrates
- ✓ Proteins
- ✓ Fats
- ✓ Vitamins

- ✓ Minerals
- ✓ Exercise and Rest

The Epilogue concludes with the need for self-awareness and a prayer for wisdom in balancing what we eat. This emphasises the fact that prevention is better than cure.

This book is not intended to send us on a guilt trip; but rather to alert us to the triple 'A's: Awake! Arise! and Act! – thus directing us to take control of our health, and not to allow our health to take control of us.

Through this book, I am inviting you readers to make a worthwhile decision, if you have not yet done so, to be in control of your health. Alternatively, I am encouraging those of us who have already done so, to be agents of encouragement to others so that they would act decisively, develop a healthy lifestyle and balance what they eat.

I must acknowledge the great efforts of the NHS in England and Wales in promoting health awareness and the billions of pounds spent for associated projects. Despite the fact that there are many books and articles that are written on health promotion, which are aptly valuable for educating us on this subject, I believe that the ideas gleaned in this book will encourage you to appreciate better living and good health.

An Essential food scenario

Every person needs food for survival. Therefore, food is the source of life. However, if we are unaware of the foods, we eat and how to balance their nutritional value in our daily intake, then food can be described as negative; a vehicle that gradually ushers life away. There may be complications when food is consumed excessively.

The following scenario relates to a true-life story. A friend I knew as a teenager was told by her General Practitioner (GP) that she was using the food she ate to dig her own grave. Indicating, that she was eating disproportionately; which was detrimental to her health. Because of this, the GP referred her to see a Dietician. The name *Pat* is used as an alias in reference to my friend.

After Pat was diagnosed as clinically obese, she became conscious of the risk of eating inconsiderately. She then proposed to educate herself on the food she eats, in terms of their nutritional values, and to discipline herself to eat wisely to be in good health.

Pat initially met with the Dietician but was baffled why her GP had made the referral. She assumes that the knowledge she had gained from parents over the years was correct. She had been brought up with the idea that food was the source of life, therefore, to eat well meant to eat what she wanted.

The Dietician explains to Pat that food may be regarded as the source for life, however; the doctor was alerting her to health risks. She told Pat that if she was not careful of the portion sizes and types of food that she was eating, then food could be harmful to her body. She also briefly defined what food is, so that Pat was aware of what she was putting into her body.

Food is usually of plant or animal origin, which consists of essential body nutrients, such as:

- ◆ Carbohydrates
- ◆ Fats
- ◆ Proteins
- ◆ Vitamins and minerals

We ingest all these, which are subsequently assimilated into us to produce energy, stimulate growth, and maintain life.

Pat was intensely upset that the doctor had described her as 'obese' and felt embarrassed by this description. The Dietician clarified that the doctor's intention was not to embarrass her. He was merely making her aware of her health status and the importance of maintaining a balanced diet as part of balancing her health.

It was difficult for Pat to understand and accept these points, as she was sticking to an ingrained perspective of what constituted a balanced diet. She was unable to grasp the concept of what constitute a 'balanced diet'. Her perception was that, eating a large variety of foods and in bulk, she was eating healthily and therefore should be doing well.

The Dietician explained that while a 'balanced diet' was fundamental to health, it was only one aspect of Pat's health.

'Health' is a state of complete physical, mental and social well-being.

A 'balanced diet' is getting the right types and amounts of foods and drinks to supply nutrition and energy for maintaining body cells, tissues, and organs. Normal growth and development is also[1] supported.

It was at that point that Pat understood why she had been referred. She asked for more information about how she could work toward losing her

---

[1] http://www.medhelp.org/medical-information/show/306/Balanced-diet

excess weight as she wanted to rid herself of the label of 'obese'.

The Dietician then gave explanation on the term 'obesity'.

Obesity is caused by the heavy accumulation of fat in your body to such a degree that it rapidly increases your risk of diseases that can damage your health and decrease your lifespan.[2] Key Facts about obesity.

---

[2] http://www.netdoctor.co.uk/health_advice/facts/obesity.htm

1. Worldwide obesity has more than doubled since 1980

2. In 2016, more than 1.9 billion adults, 18 years and over, were overweight. Of which over 650 million are obese.

3. Most of the world's population (65%) live in countries where overweight and obesity kills more people than underweight

4. 39 million children under the age of 5 were overweight or obese in 2020.

5. Over 340 million children and adolescents aged 5-19 were overweight or obese in 2016

6. Obesity is preventable.[3]

The causes of obesity maybe related to unhealthy diets, physical inactivity, or a medical condition. Those are the key factors which contribute to the following diseases in one's body.

---

[3] https://www.who.int/news-room/fact-sheets/detail/obesity-and-overweight

- Heart disease
- Cancer
- Diabetes

The Dietician advised Pat to begin a daily cycle called, '5 A Day Plus 2'.

In mathematical terms, 5 + 2 = 7. The number seven, from a Biblical perspective, symbolises completion.[4] This cycle consists of five stages which are intended to help people overcome obesity.

Cycle of '5 A Day Plus 2,'

The 5 a day eat well plate is one of the key elements of the health promotion of the (NHS).[5] Plus 2 is the combination of exercise and rest to the 5 a day eat well plate.

This cycle will require you to:

---

[4] The number 7 is a divine number symbolises completion. This number is used in various verses of the Bible to denote perfection and completion. It is imperative that we key into the blessings of our creative God who created the world in seven days and rested on the seventh day.

[5] http://www.nhs.uk/Livewell/Goodfood/Pages/eatwell- plate.aspx

- ◆ Acknowledge what you eat
- ◆ Know the nutritional values of the foods you eat
- ◆ Be aware of anticipated complications if what you are eating a balanced meal, or in appropriate amount of food or drink
- ◆ Know the nutritional values of the foods you eat
- ◆ Take control of your eating habit in addition to taking adequate exercise and rest

The consultation with the Dietician helped Pat to get past her own ingrained understanding of what a healthy diet meant. This understanding often comes from cultural, or family perspectives passed down from previous generations. However, with an increasing understanding of food and diet, many of the food myths or eating practices passed down to us, such as 'eat everything on your plate', can be damaging to our health.

Pat also benefitted from understanding that a balanced diet was part of a broader aim to balance her health in general.

In attempt to reach the state of balanced lifestyle, Pat understood that she would also need to work on the other aspect of her physical well-being, exercise while also maintaining her mental and social health.

After this discussion and equipped with a clearer understanding of food, diet and what it meant to aim for a broader, balanced health; Pat was motivated to develop a healthy eating regime. She was able to see the benefits by losing weight gradually. Pat's story is pertinent to all, irrespective of cultural backgrounds, age or status. This story inspired me to write this book as a health promotion tool, using the title: **My Food My Health**. *I hope you will also learn a valuable lesson.*

Part One
CARBOHYDRATES

The body requires energy to carry out its daily activities. Energy is derived from the foods we eat, such as:

- ◆ Carbohydrates
- ◆ Protein
- ◆ Fat

The above-mentioned nutrients provide the body with energy, which can be measured in the form of calories. Note that vitamins and minerals are also needed to break down the processing of food, whereby the body gains energy for effective functioning (metabolism).

A Healthy energy budget.

- Think about an effective financial balance between one's income and expenditure.
- Think about the need to stay out of the red - overdraft.
- So to prevent going into overdraft, an individual's daily energy intake should be equal to their daily energy expenditure. That individual's weight will remain stable. That person will not go into the red (overweight).

Therefore, an adequate carbohydrate intake can reduce problems or complications.

What are Carbohydrates?

Carbohydrates are the main source of energy for our bodies, commonly known as sugar and starch. There are three main types of carbohydrates:

- Simple starch
- Dietary fibres

Simple Carbohydrates:

The sources of simple carbohydrates are:

- Milk
- Fruits
- Sugars
- Honey
- Molasses
- White sugar
- Brown sugar

Complex carbohydrates:

The sources of Complex carbohydrates are high-fibre foods such as:

- Grains or cereals
- Root vegetables
- Rice
- Pasta
- Bread
- Dried peas
- Beans and other sources.

Dietary fibre:

Dietary fibres are water soluble. They can be obtained from:

- ◆ Whole wheat flour
- ◆ Wheat bran
- ◆ Vegetables
- ◆ Apples
- ◆ Prunes
- ◆ Pears
- ◆ Bananas

Benefits of Carbohydrates

Adequate intake of carbohydrates or starch offers several health benefits.

- ◆ A simple carbohydrate provides energy and helps to prevent ineffective breaking down of fat in the body.
- ◆ Complex carbohydrates provide energy and strength, by either elevating blood glucose levels or preventing them from decreasing. They enhance regular bowel movements and prevent constipation.
- ◆ Complex carbohydrate foods act as fuel to the body and assist in several physiological functions.
- ◆ Dietary fibre provides energy that is most beneficial for health, as they are rich sources of vitamin B.

Warning!

Deficiency of carbohydrates in your diet will cause your energy levels to be depleted or run low. If this happens, the body will function contrary to the benefits already indicated.

Analysis

Deficiency of Carbohydrates:
- ◆ You are encouraged to look at the several types of carbohydrates once again and think of how often you are, including them in your meals. Think about how your body functioned in the past when you had no carbohydrates in your meals.
- ◆ Can you think about someone you know or have seen that may not be eating sufficient carbohydrates?
- ◆ How often do you go shopping and plan so that you would balance your shopping basket with sufficient carbohydrates?
- ◆ It is important to note that deficiency of carbohydrates in one's diet causes depletion or reduction of your energy level.
- ◆ Can you remember the last time you experienced or felt that your energy level was low? Can you relate that to your diet?

If you want your body to function perfectly, consider giving your body all that it requires in terms of an essential daily quantity and quality of carbohydrates.

Now that you know how essential carbohydrates works, think about looking closely at your health and keeping a keen eye on what you eat daily.

NOTE:

Dietary fibre provides energy. It is beneficial for good health as it is a rich source of vitamin B. It also helps to improve sugar (glucose) tolerance in diabetics as they delay sugar absorption, by slowing down the emptying of the stomach.

Balancing my carbohydrate intake

Keeping a balance in whatever, we do is not an easy task, especially if your schedule is busy. Nevertheless, it is possible through discipline. Too much or too little carbohydrate in the body will lead to several complications.

Warning!

Reinstating a deficiency of carbohydrates in one's diet causes depletion of energy levels. On the other hand, carbohydrate in excess may cause the elevation of sugar levels which can be associated with the complication of sugar diabetes. It is vital for us to eat carbohydrates, but importantly, we must balance our intake.

Making sense of High- Fibre:

The essence of fibre:

In simple terms, fibre is like a thread or string, similar in function to dental floss.

What does flossing do?

Flossing helps us to remove or clear any built-up food particles which could become bacteria if it remains in our mouths for any significant period. Fibre works in a similar way, although it uses many strands to remove unnecessary waste product within the digestive system.

The reality of fibre:

Fibre cannot be digested by the body when eaten. It passes through the small intestine into the colon and then out of your body.

Fibre as Nature's scrub brush:

In my professional working environment, a scrub brush is used to enhance hand washing hygiene before surgical procedures. Scrub brushes are used to remove dirt or bacteria from the hands, especially within the nail bed, that ordinary hand washing cannot do. In a similar way, fibre acts as a scrub brush to sweep away unnecessary particles within the digestive system that a diet without fibre cannot do.

Fibre sweeps away residues:

As fibre passes through the intestine, colon, it sweeps away any rubbish that's in its path to rid it from the body. For example, while fibre cleanses the digestive system, high fibre binds with fat and toxins, assisting in cleansing the entire body. By travelling down this route, high fibre foods help in keeping your colon healthy, thus promoting regularity in the emptying of the bowel.

Health Benefits of Fibre:

The health benefits of having fibre in our diet are to reduce the risk of:

- High cholesterol
- Cardiovascular (heart) diseases
- Obesity
- Haemorrhoids
- Some forms of cancer
- High blood sugar
- Diabetes
- Becoming Overweight

If you are experiencing any of the above listed complications, I encourage you to include fibre in your diet. For any medical or nutritional advice, I encourage you to consult your General Practitioner (GP) or Nutritionist.

Sources of High- fibre:

There are five categories of high fibre foods:

- ◆ Whole grains
- ◆ Nuts and seeds
- ◆ Vegetables
- ◆ Beans and legumes

They can be obtained from: Whole wheat flour and wheat bran, vegetables, apples, prunes, pears, bananas.

Part Two
PROTEINS

Proteins like carbohydrates are essential energy giving nutrients to our daily diets. The main requirement of protein is for the formation of all body frameworks, for example, repairing and building of the body.

What are Proteins?

Proteins are regarded as an important part of every living cell in the body. They are necessary for life and play a major part in the effective functioning of the body.

Proteins build the following:

- ◆ Bones
- ◆ Tendons
- ◆ Muscles
- ◆ Blood vessels

Proteins are a component of our body fluids, such as:

- ◆ Hormones
- ◆ Enzymes
- ◆ Plasma

When portions of proteins are combined, they form building blocks of cells which are called amino acids. Proteins are labelled in two basic categories: high and low-quality protein.

High Quality Proteins

High-quality proteins are also called essential or complete proteins. They contain a sufficient amount and portion of essential building blocks known as amino acids. Amino acids provide the cells with the building materials they need to grow and maintain their structure.

Sources of high-quality proteins are animals and their products:

- ◆ Meat
- ◆ Fish
- ◆ Poultry
- ◆ Milk and milk products
- ◆ Eggs

Low-Quality proteins

Low-quality proteins are labelled incomplete or non-essential. They are lacking in one or more essential building blocks.

Sources of low-quality proteins are vegetables, fruits, grains and nuts:

- ◆ Leafy green vegetables
- ◆ Broccoli
- ◆ Nuts
- ◆ Sesame seeds
- ◆ Beans & peas
- ◆ Lentils
- ◆ Barley
- ◆ Whole grain cereals

If you are vegetarian, you can still consume high-quality proteins. For you to do so, you will need to combine certain foods that are low-quality proteins to get the full benefit. For instance, whole grain cereals eaten with beans or lentils can produce high-quality proteins. Health experts recommended that we eat more vegetable proteins and less of animal proteins.

Benefits of Proteins in our diet:
- ◆ They provide building materials for growth.
- ◆ They provide materials for tissue repair.
- ◆ Your body uses proteins to build and repair tissues.
- ◆ Enzymes, hormones and other body chemicals are products of proteins.
- ◆ Proteins are important building blocks for hair, nails, bones, muscles, cartilage, skin and blood.

Balancing your protein intake:

The saying, 'too much of one thing is good for nothing' can be linked to the overconsumption of proteins. Too much protein in the diet can result in reduced kidney functions.

High levels of protein filtered by the kidney can cause damage to the small filtering cells in the kidneys. Over a period of time, this can lead to decreased kidney functions. If your kidneys are not working well, they cannot filter protein waste products effectively.

Contrastingly, having insufficient amounts of important dietary elements can also be critical. Too little protein in the diet may lead to an imbalance of dietary needs. As a result, will lead to an imbalance in one's general health, worst-case scenario, hospitalisation is inevitable. Hence, it is important to get the right amount and the right types of protein in our diet.

Inadequate protein intake can also lead to poor nutrition that can result in muscle loss and increase the chance of infections; this can be fatal. It is, therefore, necessary to create a good balance by eating the right amount and right type of protein.

Part Three
FAT

———❤———

Fat in the diet provides energy like protein and carbohydrate. Fat is the most concentrated source of energy. Nonetheless, fat in excess in the diet can be risky for our health. Health Professional and Dieticians alike have been advocating the importance of low-fat diets. The key message in their advocacy is lowering the amount of fat we eat is the answer to:

- ◆ Losing weight
- ◆ Controlling cholesterol level
- ◆ Preventing some health issues

♦ Research states that simply cutting fat from our diet does not prove to be effective. Instead, we should consider the *type* of fats that we eat which are important.[6]

Making sense of fats

Fats can be categorised as either good fats or bad fats. Learning to use good fat instead of bad fat in our diet will contribute to better health and well-being. This is a case of knowing what to do and doing it right.

Good Fats

Good fats are called unsaturated fats. The term unsaturated means that those kinds of fats that remain liquid at room temperature and are referred to as oils. They are called good fats, as they do not clog up inside our digestive system. Most vegetable fats are considered good.

---

[6] http://www.helpguide.org/life/healthy_diet_fats.htm 20

Sources of good fats

Foods that are high in good fats include nuts, seeds and fish, including vegetable oils such as:

- ◆ Olive oil
- ◆ Canola oil
- ◆ Sunflower oil
- ◆ Soy oil
- ◆ Corn oil

Bad Fats

Bad fats are also labelled saturated fats. Saturated fats have a solid consistency at room temperature. Unlike unsaturated fats. Saturated fats become more solid and stable within the body. These kinds of fats are called 'trans-fat' and they raise the serum cholesterol level. Good fats, however, lower the serum cholesterol level.

Sources of bad fats

Foods that are high in bad fats include:

- ◆ Red meat
- ◆ Cheese
- ◆ Butter
- ◆ Ice cream
- ◆ Processed food made with trans-fat (solid fats at room temperature.)

The Waistline War with Fats

Throughout the world, there is a battle people are fighting in terms of the kind of fat that is mostly consumed. The effect of balancing our daily intake of fat in the diet is like a battle between good and bad fats. This battle is entitled: 'The Waistline War with Fat.'

There are two basic shape descriptions for waistline fat distribution in the body:

Pear-shaped body: This is where an individual is accumulates fat in the hip, buttocks, and thigh. An individual with a pear-shape will be at a lower risk of developing diabetes and heart disease.

Apple-shaped body: An individual with an apple shaped body accumulates fat mostly around the waistline/abdomen. People with apple shape are at greater risk of developing diabetes and heart disease than those with pear shape. Good fat provides energy, which is important for the body, yet energy must be consumed within reasonable balance.

Bad fat is the source of energy in high solid level. This kind of fat is not good for the body. High solid level fat within the abdominal area is unhealthy for any individual. This is why it is important to know the difference between good and bad fat.

The body requires some degree of warmth; good fat works as an insulator in maintaining body temperature and also as a cushion for internal organs.

The excessive intake of bad fat is an elevator for cholesterol serum. Our bodies require some cholesterol to function properly. It is that fat-like waxy substance found in all parts of the body. High level of cholesterol in the blood can clog or thicken the wall of your arteries. Arteries carry pure blood (oxygenated blood) to all parts of the body.

If cholesterol level is high, it will cause a narrowing of space within the arteries. This condition is likened to a drainage pipe from a kitchen sink. If grease from dirty dishes constantly flows down the drain of a sink without being treated with some chemical or boiling water, the sink will eventually become blocked.

In a similar way, if our cholesterol level increases, it will increase the risk of heart disease as there will be pressure in the arteries as the pure blood from the heart forces its way through the narrowed arteries. It is important to note that cholesterol levels increase as one becomes older or if overweight.

Cholesterol level can be lowered by eating more fruits and vegetable and by exercising (refer to the sources given for good fat).

Doctor's prescribed medicine can also lower cholesterol. High cholesterol level can be detected with a blood test as usually there may not be signs or a symptom which indicates that you have high blood cholesterol.

As you read this section, it may be possible that this is what is happening to you. Please visit your General Practitioner to have a blood test if you want to know what your cholesterol level is. Good fat helps you to reduce the risk of becoming overweight in the abdomen.

Waistline fat increases the risk of:

- ◆ Diabetes
- ◆ Obesity
- ◆ Stroke & heart attack

Good fat is the undefeated source of good health. Bad fat is the defeating source of good health.

Analysis:

Researchers have discovered that losing abdominal fat is one of the most important steps to take in maintaining physical health. The analysis of the waistline war is that fat in excess is unhealthy in the body.

Result of waist line war:

Bad fat wins: In waistline war with fat, overweight, obesity and diabetes are indication that bad fat had scored more points in this war. This is clear evidence as 65% of the world's population live in countries where more people are killed by the effects of being overweight or obese compared to the effects of being underweight.

How to arm yourself for the war

It is important in your own battle against bad fat by arming yourself properly. You can do this by:

- Undertaking regular physical exercise, ensuring you get proper rest and balancing your fat intake. Unhealthy diets and consistent physical inactivity are key risk factors for cardiovascular diseases, cancer, and diabetes.
- Replacing Bad fats with Good fats will score more points in the waistline war.
- Eating your 'five a day' is just part of the solution. We must exercise and rest also.

Warning!

Considering that obesity worldwide has doubled since 1980, there is a clear indication that the waistline war with fats is a serious matter that should not be ignored.

Health professionals, Doctors and Nutritionists:

What are we going to do about this result? Let's call for the triple 'A's: Awake, Arise and Act. 5 a day on its own will not do, as the heavyweight fighter **bad fat** is landing fatal punches on the delicate regions of the waistline. Health professionals, doctors and nutritionist are advising everyone who is concerned about their food, health, and wellbeing, to use the cycle of '5 A Day + 2', with the plus 2 as exercise and rest.

My personal experience:

Presently, my husband and I are experiencing waistline war with fats.

Yielding to temptation:

My husband is a chef and prepares tasty, spicy, delicious dishes. Oh! His dishes are appetising and mouth-watering. Because of the nature of my schedule, the ratio of my cooking is roughly 60 - 40. I have observed that my own body-shape, which was a pear-shape in my early twenties, is slowly becoming apple shaped. The very same thing is happening to my husband. We constantly reflect on how slim we were.

As a health practitioner, the knowledge of the dangers of health-risks alerted me to maintain a healthy lifestyle. In the past, I could run up the staircase and not gasp for breath. So, I told my husband that although I love his cooking, I will be in control of what we eat and drink.

A change in our lifestyles:

We are cautious of not only what we eat but also of our lifestyle. One morning, I got out of bed and thought about the '5 a day plus 2'. I am fully aware of the 5 a day as this was included frequently in our diet. However, the Plus 2 elements, I was not achieving. For days the idea 5 a day plus 2 played on my mind. I began to evaluate my life in the following areas.

Personal evaluation question:
- ◆ Am I eating healthy?
- ◆ Am I exercising daily?
- ◆ Am I getting enough rest?

If you were to give yourself a score out of ten: What would be your score? I know my score and I am still engaged in the waistline war. However, it has encouraged us both to seriously consider take into consideration, our health and wellbeing. I also considered the following questions.

- Am I setting a good example regarding my health as a nurse?
- Am I leading by example regarding my health as a minister?
- What am I going to do about my concerns regarding my own health?

Perhaps there are associated questions that you should be asking yourself. What kind of example are you showing to your children or loved ones?

I embraced the Triple A concept:

I am **awakened** to the reality that I am taking control of my health.

I **arise** to the need to preach and promote health sermons.

I am **actively** involved in health promotions.

What is your personal Triple A?

Part Four
VITAMINS

―――――――∺❤∺―――――――

Vitamins are needed for the breaking down of energy (calorie), in contrast to carbohydrates, protein and fats which produce energy. As in the comparison between energy income and expenditure: vitamins can be associated to a financial spreadsheet which reflect the details of expenditure. Vitamins, in reality, perform the actual breaking down of energy for the survival of the body.

Making Sense of Vitamins

Vitamins are essential substances that are needed in the body for growth, and development. The body requires a small number of vitamins to carry out its functions. They are present in foods in small portions. Fresh foods are higher in vitamins than processed foods. Vitamins can be destroyed by light and heat and during food preparation.

Types of Vitamins:

There are two types of vitamins:

- ◆ Fat-soluble vitamins
- ◆ Water-soluble vitamins

Fat-soluble Vitamins:

These types of vitamins are transported around the body in fat. Excess fat-soluble vitamins are stored in the liver and fatty tissues of the body. Therefore, because these get stored, the body does not require them from food sources on a daily basis.

Source of Fat-soluble vitamins (A, D, E & K)

Vitamin A:
- Liver
- Egg yolk
- Fortified milk
- Carrots

Vitamin D:
- Fish liver oils
- Sunlight
- Fortified milk

Vitamin E:
- Whole grain products
- Vegetable oils
- Wheat germs

Vitamin K:
- Dark, green leaf vegetable

Water- soluble Vitamins:

Water-soluble vitamins are transported around the body in water. As a result, these vitamins are not generally stored in the body.

Source of Water-soluble Vitamins (B & C):

Vitamin C:
- ◆ Citrus fruits
- ◆ Broccoli
- ◆ Green pepper
- ◆ Strawberries
- ◆ Greens **Vitamin B:**
- ◆ Whole and enriched grain
- ◆ Liver
- ◆ Egg yolk
- ◆ Seafood
- ◆ Yeast banana spinach
- ◆ Banana
- ◆ Kidney
- ◆ Lean meat

Benefits of Vitamins in your diet

In general, vitamins are required for the survival of the body. Other benefits to be gained from vitamins in our diets are:

- Growth and development
- Enhanced iron absorption
- Necessary for blood clotting (vitamin K)
- Carbohydrate, fat and protein breaking down for absorption.
- Visual sharpness in dim light

Complications: Insufficient Vitamins in your diet

Many studies have attempted to evaluate the relationship of vitamin intake to disease ranging from heart problems and disease of the bones. Complications such as:

- Delayed wound healing
- Delayed blood clotting
- Haemorrhaging
- Beriberi (disease caused by insufficient water-soluble vitamins in the body)
- Mental confusion
- Weakness
- Night blindness
- Rough skin
- Bone malformation
- Delayed bone growth

Balancing the intake of Vitamins:
- ◆ Eating a wide variety of fresh foods.
- ◆ Frozen vegetables are also a good option; they contain more vitamins than vegetables stored for a long time at room temperature.
- ◆ Having too many vitamins can also be dangerous. This is especially true of the fat-soluble vitamins A, D, E and K because it is much harder for the body to get rid of any excess through urine.

Deficiency of Vitamins - a Case study

For confidentiality reasons, the main characters in this case study are the Nutritionist and Mary, the mother of a six-year-old boy, John. Mary got pregnant with John at the age of seventeen. During her pregnancy, she could not tolerate some vital nutrients that would be necessary for both her and her unborn child.

After John was born, it was discovered by a Paediatrician (child doctor) that he had cleft palate and lip. This discovery was I traumatising for the teenage mother.

At the time of pregnancy, Mary could not digest certain foods that she was encouraged to eat. She was also not fully aware of the importance of taking folic acid.

Folic acid is one of the vitamin B groups. It is important during pregnancy for the creation of the baby's nervous system. It can also help to prevent inherited abnormalities - including the cleft palate (cleft lip). Good sources of folic acid are barley beans, fruit, beans, green vegetables, orange juice and peas.

Unfortunately, Mary didn't eat or couldn't digest some of the foods connected to folic acid. Her son's cleft palate may not have been caused by this, however Mary felt a sense of guilt about not paying more attention to the nutritional advice given during her pregnancy. She felt that it might have been a contributing factor to her son's condition.

A happy ending

John underwent surgical procedures to correct the deformation of his lips and palate. Mary is now a happy, well-informed mum and has forgiven herself.

Part Five
MINERALS

Vitamins help in the breaking down of energy; Minerals, on the other hand help vitamins to work. Both minerals and vitamins enhance the body's system in defence against germs and diseases. They boost the immune-system. By protecting the body, mineral and vitamins can be described as the policemen of the body. However, their functions differ in the body.

Making sense of Minerals:

Minerals are refined elements found in all parts of the body's fluids and tissues in the form of salts. They are obtained in our diets from the food we eat, as they cannot be made in the body.

Main functions of Minerals and Vitamins:

- Metabolic functions – helping the physical aspects of health
- Mental development
- Structural support functions and social aspects of health

Metabolic functions:

Metabolic functions refer to the physical process whereby the body breaks down food. There are two phases within the breaking-down process namely:

- Assimilation
- Absorption

For example, if you are given a jig-saw puzzle to fit, the first thing you will do is to assemble the pieces in their right places.

Assimilation and absorption:

- Carbohydrate, proteins and fats are eaten
- The body receives energy

◆ Vitamins are required in the diet to breakdown the energy in preparation for absorption
◆ Minerals are needed in the diet to break down vitamins so that the food will be absorbed by the body
◆ Metabolic functions in the body can be associated with a state of physical well-being.

Mental development:

The development of mental functions relates to normal brain functions and the health of the brain cells. Vitamins and minerals are vital in this process.

Health professionals suggested the following:[7]

◆ That the presence of vitamin E supports the protection of cells, which results in the loss of fewer brain cells.
◆ That there are many vitamin D receptors in the brain, which are involved in learning and memory.

---

[7] Read more:
http://www.livestrong.com/article/409409-3-most-common-functions-of-vitamins-minerals/
#ixzz1nzrWtrSL

Structural Support Functions

The structure support functions are actually the framework of the body. This is essential for movement and development within those areas. Vitamins and minerals are important for maintaining healthy bones and teeth.

- ◆ Bones serves as mineral storage sites for the body.
- ◆ Vitamin D is needed in our diet for the body to be able to absorb calcium.

Vitamins and minerals complement each other. When this complimentary state is well balanced, it brings a lot of good to our body.

Classification of Minerals:

Dietary minerals are divided into two categories by health professionals, namely:

- ◆ Major Minerals
- ◆ Trace minerals

Major minerals are:
- Calcium
- Magnesium
- Chloride phosphorus
- Potassium
- Sodium

Trace minerals:
- Copper
- Iodine
- Iron

Major minerals:
- Whole grains (potassium)
- Fruits (potassium)
- Milk and milk products (phosphorous)
- Green leafy vegetables (magnesium)
- Salt (sodium/ chloride)

Trace minerals
- Iodised salt (Iodine)
- Liver (iron)
- Dried peas and beans

Salt:

Salt is a key ingredient in the preparation of almost every dish. I have briefly given some facts about salt it under three sub-headings:

- ◆ What is salt?
- ◆ The importance of salt in our diet
- ◆ Reducing salt intake in our diet

What is Salt?

Salt is known to be a chemical mixture that is made up of sodium/chloride, which is a major mineral our body needs to:

- Maintain fluid balance
- Maintain blood pressure.

Three basic types of salt are:
- Table salt
- Iodised Sea salt
- Sea salt

Table Salt is one of the most widely used salts. The refining process that it goes through removes traces of naturally occurring minerals. Because of its fine-grained texture, it is often the preferred choice for baking. Table salt may not be the e best salt to use in our diet.

Iodised salt is a form of table salt that has had iodine added. **Sea salt** is made from evaporated sea water. It is made up of several naturally present trace minerals, including iodine, magnesium and potassium. Sea salt is more expensive than table and iodised salt. It has a fresher and lighter flavour than table salt.

The importance of salt in our diet:

Salt is important in one's body as it helps to carry out and control many of our body functions. A small amount of salt is required in the body as it assists in the control of the correct volume of blood circulation and tissue fluids in the body. It also:

- Triggers the thirst system in the body, which stimulates us to drink much needed water.
- Stimulates muscle contraction, which helps us to prevent cramps.
- Enhances food flavour. Salt allows your taste buds to taste food better; it activates an enzyme (protein) in the mouth called salivary amylase.
- Helps to break down foods in digestion
- Is useful for preservation
- Maintains the source of sodium in your diet

Complications of high Salt intake:

As explained earlier, salt is a component of sodium and most of our body's sodium intake is from salt. Sodium is a major mineral that our body needs to maintain fluid balance and blood pressure. [8]

Sodium in excess will increase the risk of:

- ◆ Hypertension (high blood pressure) – also being described as 'the silent killer'.
- ◆ Type 2 diabetes
- ◆ Disease of the Gallbladder
- ◆ Some forms of cancer
- ◆ Obesity

Taking too much salt triggers thirst, which encourages many to consume fluids such as beers or sodas, which are high in calories. This will result in excess weight-gain and obesity.

---

[8] http://www.helpguide.org/life/healthy_diet_fats.htm
Encyclopedia of Natural Medicine, 2nd Edition;
Michael Murray, N.D., Joseph Pizzorno, N.D.; 1998
http://nutrition.about.com/od/mineralglossary/g/sodiumglossary.htm

With the details given on salt, the following questions are formulated to help evaluate our salt intake.

Evaluation of your salt intake:
- ◆ Which one of the salts mentioned is best for your dietary intake?
- ◆ Why do you believe that the one you have chosen is the best?
- ◆ Is the type of salt you have chosen the one you are presently using in your food preparations?
- ◆ If 'yes,' will you continue to use it?
- ◆ If 'no' have you learnt something new that will cause you to change the type of salt that you are currently using?
- ◆ Looking at the benefits and complications shown so far, do you think you need to reduce your salt intake?

Reducing your Salt intake:

If you are engaged in cooking, you will be aware that adding salt, enhance the flavour of your food. However, healthy eating and providing healthy meals for your family and loved ones involves not only the flavour of the dishes, but also making healthy choices.

Quite often when food is being prepared, salt is added. Very often, I observed friends and loved ones before they taste their meals; they chose to add salt to it. This could be an unhealthy habit.

The following tips that can help you to reduce salt in food preparation.

- ◆ Use herbs and spices such as garlic and lemon juice to add flavour to meals.
- ◆ Avoid adding salt to cooking and at the table.
- ◆ Note that salt is already added to some spices and seasoning; so use salt sparingly.
- ◆ Buy varieties of sauces, spices and ingredients that are salt free or of low salt content.
- ◆ For your cooking, use fresh or frozen vegetables rather than those that have been canned.

It may be difficult to break old habits, or change is not always easy. However, I encourage you to lessen your salt intake gradually. Give yourself time, for your tastebuds too become accustomed to a lower level of salt in your food. There are groups of people that are at a higher risk of high blood pressure, due to cultural food practices and physical characteristics. For example, the African-Caribbean communities tend to suffer from a higher incidence of salt sensitivity and higher sodium retention in comparison to other groups. Sodium retention can increase the risk of high blood pressure and heart disease, stroke, or even death.

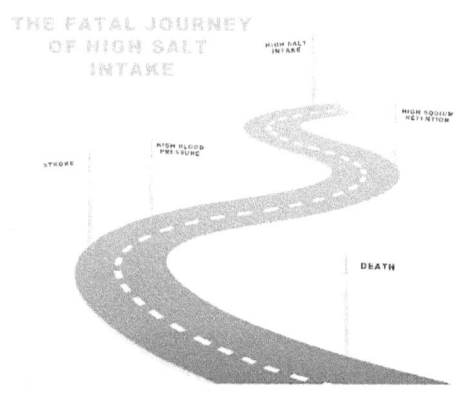

Part Six
EXERCISE & REST

Exercise and rest are two vital elements that the human body was designed to take. It is sad that in the fast pace of life, many of us are finding it difficult to rest. Regular exercise and rest are important for the healthy functioning of the body. They are essential for health promotion strategies. The well publicised 5 a day healthy plate is of no effect without exercise and rest.

Health risks of inadequate exercise and rest

Individuals that operate a busy schedule will easily identify themselves on this page – admitting that they are guilty of inadequate exercise and rest. If caution is not regarded, they will soon find out that those who do not rest also suffer like those who do not eat well. For example:

- ◆ Individuals who choose inactive lifestyle
- ◆ People who are inactive because of illness or injury
- ◆ Individuals whose body doesn't get enough rest

The health risks differ in terms of age and the physical status for those individuals.

Exploring the holistic components of humanity

The holistic aspects of humanity are body, mind, and spirit. The complete cycle of health and wellbeing is dieting, exercise and rest. Each of the three components is dependent on each other.

The Concept of Exercise

Exercise is the physical exertion of the body. In process, the body does physical activities that result in a healthy or healthier level of physical and mental fitness. [9] In this definition, exercise is regarded as a physical activity which is a vital element for every living being because the body is designed for movement and activity.

Therefore, the aim of exercise is:
- ◆ To maintain physical fitness
- ◆ To enhance physical fitness

The words **maintain** and **enhance** indicate the purposes for which we exercise.

Fitness Facilities

Many people have come to realise that exercise is very important for their well-being. That is why Gyms have become so popular. Many organisations are now encouraging their members to be actively involved in the exercising regimes.

---

[9] http://www.medicalnewstoday.com/articles/153390.php

Government Agenda on Fitness:

Post COVID-19, the Government of the United Kingdom has been promoting the need for communities and people of all ages to be actively involved in exercises. There are dedicated Leisure and Community Centres that have Gyms and Swimming Pools. I have also intensified my keeping fit activities.

A Nurse's advice on fitness:

It is recommended that one should not pursue fitness without seeking medical help or guidance. The reason for the encouragement is that there may be unknown health conditions that require medical advice. Speaking to many patients over the years, I have discovered that some have damaged their health because of not consulting a medical professional before taking on a new physical fitness regime. As a result, I encourage you to do so.

Please have conversations with your health providers before embarking on any intense exercise. Leisure Centres also take time to instruct those who seek to use their facilities.

My Personal Experience in fitness

In my early teenage years up until my early twenties, my major type of exercise was athletics. I was able to gain the skills of endurance during long distance races.

Benefits: Body
- ◆ I maintained my body weight
- ◆ I maintained the activity of my body's muscles

The ideology of 'no gain without pain,' in fact, led to some of the injuries I sustained during practice and in the actual track and field events. Therefore, this mantra should be avoided, especially if one is returning to exercise after a long period. The positive effects gained outweighed the injuries that I had sustained.

Benefits: Mind
- ◆ The opportunity to socialise

- ◆ I Learned how to cope well with competition pressures
- ◆ I Learned how to remain positive in defeat and humble in victory
- ◆ I Learned the discipline of endurance

Benefits: Spirit

The context in which I use the word spirit implies an aspiration to the real meaning and purpose of life. In this stage, benefits related to my faith in a supreme being and the conclusion that there is more to me as:

- ◆ I became capable of defying predictable problems through my faith in God.
- ◆ I learned to understand that within me there is power to demonstrate that I can do all things through Christ who strengthens me (Philippians 4:13)
- ◆ I learned to remain focused amidst the challenges or distractions that surround me.

As I become older, the purpose of exercise became clearer, especially in the areas of maintaining and enhancing my health.

Types of Exercises:

There are three main types of exercises, namely:

Light exercise: An example of this is going for a walk; during this type of exercise, the individual is able to talk.

Moderate exercise: During this type of exercise, depending on your level of fitness, the exerciser will feel a sense of breathlessness or be slightly out of breath. The heart beats faster during this type of exercise, resulting in breathlessness. An example of this exercise is walking briskly.

Vigorous exercise: In the process of this type of exercise, it's as though the body is being pushed to its limit. Note that the body will cope or fail to do so, depending on the individual's level of fitness. Endurance will be built as a result of this type of exercise. Examples are heavy weight training, running, or cycling fast.

Note:

For the fit person, the three types of exercises may be recommended.

Exercises for the Immobile/ Sick Person:

Professional advice is highly recommended in the case of a sick or immobile person.

The following scenario outlines a consultation between a nurse and a patient. This explains the nursing process for mobility and exercise.

Nurse: What type of physical exercise would you do on a daily routine and how often?

Patient/ Client: Usually I am able to do all basic home duties, including shopping.

Nurse: Are there any changes in what you normally do and how do those changes affect you?

Patient/client: There are changes as I am not able to do my shopping due to the feeling of breathlessness walking about for any period of time. This happened recently and it is affecting me whenever I climb the stairs.

Nurse: Are you currently on any exercise programme and how do you feel about that?

Patient/client: I am not on any programme at present, as I am quite apprehensive. I'm worried that exercising will cause my breathing to get worse.

Nurse: I do understand how you are feeling based on your experiences; however, you will not be left alone to do this. You will be guided by an experienced person and the aim of it will be to help you to overcome that breathing problem.

Patient/ client: As long as somebody with experience is available to guide me through that programme, I will have a try, as I want to get better.

Nurse: Is there any other problem you can think of that contributes to this problem?

Patient/client: I don't know if the pace-maker the doctor put in my heart some years ago may be contributing to how I am feeling.

Nurse: Thanks for letting me know this. Your doctor will be able to tell you more about that. I will book an appointment for him to speak with you talk with you later.

Conclusion of scenario:

The patient was placed on a mild physical exercising programme, which he said was beneficial to his health.

Listen to your Body

The body is the temple that houses your spirit and soul. It will respond to whatever treatment we give to it. More than what our Doctors can do, we need to listen to our bodies. It is the body that alerts us to the need for a physician. The body alerts us to the need for food, water, shelter, and rest.

Making sense of rest:

With reference to the Bible, rest simply means to cease from hectic or unnecessary activities.

On the seventh day God ended His work, which He had made and rested (Genesis 2: 2)

Rest for me is more than the Dictionary's definition, but rather a lived experience that is essential to building the body in the following ways:

- ◆ Refreshing
- ◆ Revitalising
- ◆ Restoring
- ◆ Replenishing

- Renewing
- Recharging

The human body requires balance in eating healthily and having adequate exercise and rest to function effectively.

The Body is designed to rest

The vital organs of our body are skilfully and intelligently designed with a built-in period for rest.

- The lungs rest between each breath
- The heart rests between each beat
- The stomach rests between each meal
- The central nervous system is recharged during sleep

If our body is not getting enough rest, it will go into over-drive. By this I mean it will develop complications that are threatening to our health. For example, lack of rest will lead to a state of:

- Restlessness
- Sleeplessness

- Wakefulness

Benefits of Rest and Relaxation

Whenever our body rests or relaxes, we get the opportunity to unwind and recuperate. Researched benefits of relaxation are:

- Reduced blood pressure
- Increased blood flow to the muscles
- Heart rate slowed down
- Slowdown of breathing, which reduces the need for oxygen

Body's response to Rest-Relaxation
- More energy
- Better sleep
- Enhanced immunity
- Better problem-solving abilities
- Increased level of concentration

Warning!

With the natural need of our body to rest, we do not need to make excuses to rest. Do not feel guilty about saying, "I am taking time for rest." Failure to do so will lead to a premature end to our lifespan. I am writing this important message to all readers with no exception. We must all rest and receive the full benefits.

Resting the Body

The proverb; 'Rome wasn't built in a day', relates to the importance of adding rest to our daily lifestyle. Exercise contributes to healthy living and promotes rest. From a personal experience, whenever I exercise I get a good night's sleep.

The importance of sleep Researchers have stated that lack of sleep may lead to type 2 diabetes. This is caused by the effects of how the body processes glucose. Sleep, therefore, reduces the risk of diabetes. Having insufficient sleep may also lead to mood swings.

For example, having sleepless nights may cause agitation, or one becoming moody. Lack of sleep for a long period studies have shown, can lead to long-term mood disorders such as depression or anxiety.

The benefits of sleep are extensive and can make a difference in your quality of life. As a result, is vital to place priority on getting adequate, consistent sleep.

Tips: resting the body:
- ◆ Be realistic in organising your daily scheduled
- ◆ Pace yourself in doing your daily activities
- ◆ Set goals
- ◆ Ensure that you get adequate sleep daily
- ◆ Avoid burnt-outs

Tips: resting the Mind
- ◆ Pray and meditate
- ◆ Resolve conflicts as soon as possible
- ◆ Think positive
- ◆ Avoid becoming angry or bitter

The importance of exercise and rest should not be ignored from our daily living.

Part Seven
EPILOGUE

———— ııღıı ————

From what had been discussed in this book, it is obvious that food is the primary source of survival. Food must be consumed with a self-awareness as to:

- ◆ What we eat
- ◆ How we eat
- ◆ When we eat
- ◆ Why we eat
- ◆ Why our body needs exercise
- ◆ Why we need to take rest

The points listed are all answered in the pages of this book; nevertheless, it is important to develop a personal awareness of how to promote a healthy lifestyle.

Making sense of Self-awareness

Self-awareness is having an understanding of your personality and understanding of other people, thus:

- ◆ How they perceive you
- ◆ Your attitude and response to them

For example, the scenario given in the Prologue reflects Pat's perception, attitude and response towards her General Practitioner when she was diagnosed as being clinically obese. Her impression was that her doctor embarrassed her. An improved self-awareness with regards to Pat would mean that she becomes Awake, Alert and ready to Act.

I suggest that you see Appendix 1 and plan what you need to do in order to create a healthier balance for your life. I do acknowledge that we are living in a society where the health of people is at risk of serious complications. The influence on this comes from a combination of various factors, such as:

- ◆ Physical
- ◆ Psychological
- ◆ Socio-cultural
- ◆ Environmental
- ◆ Politico-economic

You may be asking: If I follow a healthy lifestyle, will I sustain good health through my lifespan? The answer is a resounding YES. Good health will be guaranteed if you maintain a positive lifestyle.

An intercessory prayer for wisdom:

I conclude this book with an intercessory prayer for us to gain wisdom:

Oh Lord my God; Creator of all mankind, thank you for the gift of life. I acknowledge that there is a time limit to our physical existence. The desire of my heart is to gain wisdom so that I can guide others to live a healthy lifestyle within their lifespan on earth.

As in the Holy Scriptures (Job 28:12-28) the quest for wisdom, so is this prayer:

I ask that you will give us wisdom to balance our daily intake of food.

Lord, let the manifestation of wisdom in our lives be fortified with grace, love, and mercy.

Lord, demolish the power of greed out of the lives of those who are possessed by it, through Godly wisdom and love for all humanity.

The prayer of my heart is that we will not only remember those who are poor, malnourished and starving but to give assistance wherever possible.

Grant us wisdom to give thanks for the breath that we enjoy, the sunlight, the rain, the heat and the cold. I pray that we will not only accept that our bodies were designed for movement and activity but that we will take the time to daily establish a lifestyle for exercise and rest.

Lord, let your wisdom, accompanied by peace, penetrate the lives of those who are sick, cast-down, and afflicted. This is so that they would realise that the sufferings of this world are not worthy to be compared with the glory that shall be revealed in those who are able to overcome the distractions of this life. Lord, through the company of wisdom and peace; remind us that there is more to us than food, the inner man: The soul, which can only be satisfied through the wisdom of God.

Lord gives us wisdom to live in peace and harmony with each other. Allow humankind to value the source of wisdom that comes from you.

Lord, I acknowledge that wisdom cannot be purchased with money, neither can a price-tag be placed upon it.

I admit that wisdom out-values the price of gold or sapphire. Lord, you prepare and declare wisdom to humanity in these words:

'The fear of the Lord heralds wisdom,' Amen!!!

LAUREL WOODSTOCK

Framing an Action Plan: For a Healthy Lifestyle

A balanced diet, exercise and adequate rest are the holistic approach towards a healthy lifestyle.

Table 1
Analysis Action Plan Timescale

How do you plan to maintain a healthy lifestyle? What are your **strengths**?

How would you overcome **challenges** to promote a healthy lifestyle?

What are your **opportunities** in terms of healthy eating, exercise and rest in promoting a healthy lifestyle?

What are the **threats** that will hinder you from balancing your dietary intake, exercising daily, and having adequate rest? How would you overcome them?

Personal Reflection

1. What are your personal reflective notes based on issues highlighted in this book?

2. The reader's resolutions – the reader may be thinking of making positive changes after reading this book. What are they?

3. List issues you might like to discuss with a medical doctor, nurse or nutritionist.

4. Areas where you might be winning and eating right.

5. Areas where you are losing the battle and eating wrong foods.

6. Readers may include stories that you would like to share with others about how you managed to conquer your bad eating habits.

Quick Personal Assessment

On a scale of one to ten, how well are you doing with the following?

(1=very poor 10 = Very well)

Carbohydrates

Proteins

Fat

Vitamins

Minerals

Exercise & rest

Thank you for reading *My Food My Health.*

www.marciampublishing.com

www.ingramcontent.com/pod-product-compliance
Lightning Source LLC
LaVergne TN
LVHW022112080426
835511LV00007B/769